125 Homemade Salad Dressings

Healthy And Yummy Salad & Vinaigrette Recipes

MAY ORTIZ

ISBN-13:978-1546465447

ISBN-10:1546465448

DEDICATION

To those who love good food

TABLE OF CONTENTS

INTRODUCTION

Salads are healthy foods and as such should be accompanied with a healthy dressing. The reverse is the case as many packaged dressings contain unhealthy saturated fats, hidden sugar and too much sodium. This is not good for unsuspecting consumers who try to follow a modern dietary lifestyle. However, when you make your own dressing, you are in charge of the ingredients that are used. Homemade salad dressings are wholesomely nutritious and unbelievably simple to make. They give life to your meals and make them more appealing.

Salad dressing is simply a condiment primarily used to enhance the flavor as well as texture of a salad. Bases for salad dressing include oils, mayonnaise and dairy products such as yogurt and cream. There are a vast array of dressings all over the world and some are specific to certain cultures, e.g. The Greek are known for their blend of dill, cucumber, yogurt, and lemon juice to dress simple salads. The vinaigrette is widely used in France and Italy. A dressing can include fresh herbs or pickled vegetables; vinegar or soy sauce, dried fruit or fresh ones and nuts. Other condiments, such as ketchup, can also be included. To make spicy dressings, chilies can be added and if you like it sweet; sugar and molasses.

Dressings can be thick and creamy, such as blue cheese as well as ranch dressings, which use a dairy base. They can also be light and runny. It isn't all about salads, however. Many dressings can also be used as dips for bread, as well as sauces and marinades for meat or fish. You can even use them on a sandwich. To combine all of the ingredients, you must shake before use and refrigerate when not in use so they can maintain their freshness and coolness.

The dressings in this book have been put together to suit every taste. They are also easy to modify to your unique needs. Make meal times more appealing by trying any of the versions to reflect various tastes. Your salad is not just complete without it!

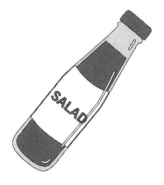

PALEO

Tarragon-Shallot Vinaigrette

Savor this chic French dressing with a flute of champagne or French bread.

Preparation time: 10 minutes

Yields: 2 cups

Ingredients:

1 cup extra-virgin olive oil

½ cup of champagne vinegar

¼ cup of fresh tarragon, roughly chopped

2 tablespoons of fresh lemon juice

1 teaspoon of Dijon mustard

4 garlic cloves, crushed

2 medium-sized shallot, crushed

1 teaspoon sea salt

¼ teaspoon black pepper

Directions:

1. In a medium bowl, whisk together the lemon juice, mustard, garlic, salt and pepper.

2. Add the vinegar, tarragon, and shallots.

3. Add the oil slowly while whisking and shake well.

White And Red Balsamic Vinaigrette

A tasty and ingenious mixture of white and red balsamic vinegar.

Preparation time: 5 minutes

Yields: 2 cups

Ingredients:

1½ cup of extra-virgin olive oil

¼ cup of white balsamic vinegar

¼ cup of red balsamic vinegar

1 teaspoon of Dijon mustard

2 cloves of garlic, crushed

1 teaspoon of salt

Dash of black pepper

Directions:

1. Whisk together the lemon juice, mustard, garlic, salt and pepper in a medium-sized bowl.

2. Add the oil slowly while whisking and shake well.

Ginger- Carrot Dressing
An Asian-inspired light salad dressing.

Preparation time: 10 minutes

Cooking time: 0 minutes

Yields: 1¾ cups

Ingredients:

¼ cup of fresh ginger, peeled and chopped

½ pound of carrots, roughly chopped

¼ cup of seasoned rice vinegar

½ cup of oil or water

2 tablespoons of chopped onion

1 tablespoon of sesame oil

1 tablespoon of soy sauce

1/8 teaspoon of salt

Directions:

1. In a food processor, pulse the carrots until it is mostly smooth.

2. Add the rest of the ingredients except the water or oil and run the processor again.

3. Add half of the oil or water and pulse the ingredients together.

4. Add the remaining oil or water slowly while running the processor until it turns smooth and looks like a sauce.

Lime-Tangerine Balsamic Dressing
A delicious balsamic dressing suitable for your paleo salads.

Preparation time: 2 minutes

Yields: ¼ cup

Ingredients:

Juice from half a lime

Juice from half a tangerine

1 tablespoon of balsamic vinegar

1 tablespoon of olive oil

Directions:

In a small bowl, whisk together all the ingredients until they are fully combined.

Italian Vinaigrette

This recipe is sugar-free, gluten-free and dairy-free.

Preparation time: 5 minutes

Yields: 2 cups

Ingredients:

1 cup of olive oil

¾ cup of red wine vinegar

2 tablespoons of dried onion flakes

2 tablespoons of Dijon mustard

I small-sized shallot, finely diced

1 garlic clove, crushed

1½ teaspoon of Italian seasoning

1½ teaspoon of garlic salt

1½ teaspoon of red pepper flakes

Directions:

Add all the ingredients to a small jar or bowl. Shake or whisk together.

Fresh Strawberry Dressing

This yummy recipe can be used in yoghurts and as an ice-cream topping.

Preparation time: 5 minutes

Yields: 1¼ cups

Ingredients:

1 cup of fresh strawberries

2 tablespoons of olive oil

1 tablespoon of balsamic vinegar

1 tablespoon of cane sugar

¼ teaspoon of sea salt

Directions:

1. In a bowl, combine the berries, vinegar and cane sugar. Allow to sit for 60 minutes.

2. Add the oil and salt and pulse in a food processor or blender.

Tomato Vinaigrette

This delicious and creamy tomato dressing can also be used as a marinade.

Preparation time: 5 minutes

Yields: 2 cups

Ingredients:

3 Roma tomatoes, seeded and chopped

¾ cup of olive oil

¼ cup of red wine vinegar

2 tablespoons of fresh basil or 1 teaspoon of dried basil

1 tablespoon of Dijon mustard

1 ½ teaspoons of liquid smoke

Salt

Pepper

Directions:

1. Blend all the ingredients in a high-speed until it is creamy and smooth.

2. Season with salt and pepper.

Mango Vinaigrette

Another use for your delicious mangoes!

Preparation time: 10 minutes

Yields: 2- 2½ cups

Ingredients:

2 ripe mangoes, peeled, chunked and pit removed

2 jalapenos, ribbed, seeded and chopped

¼ cup of extra-virgin olive oil

2 tablespoons of raw honey

1 tablespoon of white wine vinegar

Juice of 1 lemon

Sea salt

Pepper

Directions:

1. Pulse the mango, jalapenos, honey, vinegar, and lemon juice in a blender until it is smooth.

2. While the blender is still running, drizzle in the olive oil.

3. Season with salt and pepper.

Almond-Coconut Dressing

A delicious and creamy paleo dressing recipe.

Preparation time: 5 minutes

Yields: 1½ - 2 cups

Ingredients:

½ cup of almond butter

½ cup of coconut milk

2 tablespoons of warm water

2 tablespoons of cilantro, chopped finely

2 tablespoons of mint, chopped finely

Juice of 2 limes

¼ teaspoon of red pepper flakes

Salt

Directions:

1. In a bowl, whisk together the almond butter, warm water and lime juice until it is smooth.

2. Add the rest of the ingredients and stir until it becomes even.

Avocado Dressing

Use up your ripe avocados to make this creamy goodness.

Preparation time: 5 minutes

Yields: 2½ cups

Ingredients:

1 large and ripe avocado

3 garlic cloves

1 jalapeno, stemmed and seeded

1 handful of fresh cilantro

¼ cup of olive oil

¼ cup of water

2 tablespoons of apple cider vinegar

1 tablespoon of honey

Juice of 1 lime

Directions:

Put all the ingredients in a food processor or blender and allow it run until it becomes totally smooth and creamy.

Italian Dressing

A creamy version of the Italian dressing.

Preparation time: 5 minutes

Yields: 1/3 – ½ cup

Ingredients:

¼ cup of olive oil mayo

2 tablespoons of vinegar

½ teaspoon of minced garlic

½ teaspoon of dried Italian herb blend

Salt

Ground black pepper

Directions:

1. Crush the herbs using your fingers in a small bowl. Add mayo and garlic and blend thoroughly with a fork.

2. While still using the fork, drizzle in the vinegar.

3. Taste and season with salt and pepper.

Chipotle Balsamic Vinaigrette

Quick, easy, and spicy.

Preparation time: 5 minutes

Yields: ¾ - 1 cup

Ingredients:

¼ cup of balsamic vinegar

¼ cup of extra-virgin olive oil

¼ cup of garlic-infused olive oil

2 teaspoons of honey

½-1 teaspoon of chipotle chili flakes

Sea salt

Freshly ground pepper

Directions:

Add all the ingredients to a jar with a lid and shake until it is thoroughly mixed.

Easy Salad Dressing
Paleo salad dressings do not get simpler than this.

Preparation time: 15 minutes

Yields: 1¾ - 2 cups

Ingredients:

1 cup of extra-virgin olive oil

¼ cup of balsamic vinegar

1 tablespoon of lemon juice

1 medium-sized clove of garlic, finely minced

1 teaspoon of raw honey

1 teaspoon of Dijon mustard

1 teaspoon of your choice herbs

1 teaspoon of sea salt

½ teaspoon of freshly ground black pepper

Directions:

1. Put all the ingredients except the olive oil, herbs, salt and pepper in a small bowl or blender and combine thoroughly.

2. Add the oil slowly while still mixing.

3. Season with the herbs, salt and pepper.

Paleo Caesar Dressing

This recipe tastes just like the traditional Caesar dressing.

Preparation time: 10 minutes

Yields: ¾ cup

Ingredients:

½ cup of extra-virgin olive oil

1 large egg yolk

3 large cloves of garlic, peeled

4 anchovy fillets

Juice of 1 lemon

1 teaspoon of Dijon mustard

1 teaspoon of coconut amino

Salt

Pepper

Directions:

1. Put garlic and anchovies in a food processor and pulse. Add the egg yolk to the mixture and pulse.

2. Slowly add the olive oil and lemon juice.

3. Add in the mustard, coconut amino, salt, and pepper. Combine together.

Paleo Ranch Dressing

The paleo version of the famous ranch dressing.

Preparation time: 5 minutes

Yields: 2 cups

Ingredients:

1 cup of Paleo mayonnaise

¼ cup of full fat coconut milk

2 tablespoons of fresh herbs, minced

2 tablespoons of lemon juice

1 garlic clove, crushed

Sea salt

Freshly cracked black pepper

Directions:

Add all the ingredients to a bowl and whisk until it is thoroughly mixed.

Hot Bacon Vinaigrette

Yet another reason to love bacon.

Preparation time: 5 minutes

Yields: ¼ cup

Ingredients:

3 tablespoons of reserved bacon drippings

2 tablespoons of red wine vinegar

1 tablespoon of raw honey

Pinch of red pepper flakes

Sea salt

Pepper

Directions:

Add all the ingredients to a jar with a lid and shake until it is thoroughly mixed.

Maple Balsamic Vinaigrette

This recipe can also be used as a dipping sauce.

Preparation time: 5minutes

Yields: ½ cup

Ingredients:

¼ cup of balsamic vinegar

2 tablespoons of extra-virgin olive oil

1½ tablespoons of jalapeno

1 teaspoon of maple syrup

1/8 teaspoon of cayenne pepper, optional

3 pinches of salt

5 grinds of black pepper.

Directions:

1. Add all the ingredients to a jar with a lid or a bowl and shake or whisk until it is thoroughly mixed.

1. While still shaking or whisking, drizzle in the oil slowly until it is well-mixed.

French Dressing

This recipe comes with an American twist.

Preparation time: 5 minutes

Yields: 2½ - 3 cups

Ingredients:

1 cup of olive oil

¼ cup of tomato paste

½ cup of apple cider vinegar

¼ cup of honey

1/3 cup of onion, chopped

2 fresh garlic cloves

2 teaspoons of coconut amino

1 tablespoon of lemon juice

2 teaspoons of Dijon mustard

Pinch of cloves, optional

½ teaspoon of molasses, optional

1 teaspoon of salt

½ teaspoon of pepper

Directions

Put all the ingredients in a food processor and allow it run until it becomes totally smooth.

Green Salad Dressing

This recipe contains healthy fats and is also dairy-free.

Preparation time: 10 minutes

Yields: 2¼ - 2½ cups

Ingredients:

½ cup of fresh parsley, coarsely chopped

½ cup of extra-virgin olive oil

¼ cup of fresh basil, coarsely chopped

½ of a ripe avocado

¼ cup of coconut milk

3 tablespoons of lemon juice, freshly squeezed

1 tablespoon of fresh tarragon, coarsely chopped

2 anchovy fillets, finely diced

1 clove of garlic, finely diced

¼ teaspoon of salt

Directions:

1. Put all the ingredients except the olive oil in a food processor and allow it run.

2. Add the oil slowly while the processor is running. Stop when the herbs are chopped finely and the dressing becomes thick.

Ginger Dressing

A multi-purpose dressing that adds color to your salads.

Preparation time: 15 minutes

Yields: 1½ - 2 cups

Ingredients:

½ cup of light-tasting olive oil

1 tablespoon of fresh ginger, grated with skin on

1 tablespoon of coconut aminos

2 medium-sized carrots, washed and chunked

2 garlic cloves

¼ of apple cider vinegar

¼ of a medium yellow onion

Salt

Pepper

Directions:

1. In a food processor, pulse the oil, coconut aminos, and vinegar a few times.

2. Add in the onions and carrots and continue pulsing until it is mostly smooth.

3. Next, add the garlic and ginger and pulse again until the mixture is thoroughly combined.

Tzatziki Sauce

Add a touch of Greek cuisine to your salads.

Preparation time: 10 minutes

Yields: 1½ - 1¾ cups

Ingredients:

1 cup of cucumber, seeded and shredded

2 tablespoons of lemon juice

1 tablespoon of fresh dill

½ cup of full-fat coconut milk

2 cloves of garlic, minced

1/8 teaspoon of sea salt

1/8 teaspoon of black pepper

Directions:

Whisk all the ingredients together in a medium bowl until it is well-mixed.

Meyer Lemon Vinaigrette

The champagne vinegar adds a fancy dimension to this recipe.

Preparation time: 10 minutes

Yields: 1¾ - 2 cups

Ingredients:

1 cup of extra-virgin olive oil

½ cup of freshly squeezed Meyer lemon juice

¼ cup of champagne vinegar

1 tablespoon of minced shallot

1 garlic clove, minced

1 teaspoon of Dijon mustard

½ teaspoon of salt

Dash of black pepper

Directions:

1. In a medium-sized bowl, whisk together the lemon juice, mustard and salt. Then whisk in the vinegar.

2. While still whisking, drizzle in the olive oil slowly and stir in the shallot and garlic.

Peanut Dressing

A creamy dressing made with inspiration from Thai cuisine.

Preparation time: 5 minutes

Yields: 1 cup

Ingredients:

¼ cup of sunflower seed butter

¼ cup of water

3 tablespoons of honey

2 tablespoons of lemon juice, fresh

2 tablespoons of extra-virgin olive oil

1 tablespoon of tamari sauce

1 inch knob of ginger, peeled and chopped

2 cloves of garlic, crushed

¼ teaspoon of salt

¼ teaspoon of crushed red pepper flakes

Directions:

Put all the ingredients in a high-powered blender and allow it run until it becomes totally smooth.

Honey-Mustard Dressing

A perfect mix of sweet and tangy.

Preparation time: 5 minutes

Yields: ¼ cup

Ingredients:

2 tablespoons of raw honey

4 tablespoons of Dijon mustard

½ teaspoons of ginger powder

½ teaspoons of apple cider vinegar

Directions:

In a bowl, whisk all the ingredients.

Maple Mustard Dressing

Upgrade your salad from average to perfect with this thick and creamy treat.

Preparation time: 5 minutes

Yields: 2¼ - 2½ cups

Ingredients:

1 cup of raw cashews

¾ cup of warm water

5 tablespoons of apple cider vinegar

3 tablespoons of maple syrup

2 tablespoons of mustard

2 large cloves of garlic

½ teaspoon of salt

¼ teaspoon of pepper

Directions:

Put all the ingredients in a high-powered blender and allow it run until it becomes totally smooth.

FRUIT SALAD DRESSING

Fresh Salad Dressing

This recipe is ideal for stewed or fresh fruit.

Preparation time: 2 minutes

Yields: 1 cup

Ingredients:

1 cup of low-fat plain yoghurt

½ teaspoon of fresh lemon rind, grated

¼ teaspoon of ginger

¼ teaspoon of nutmeg

¼ teaspoon of cinnamon

Directions:

Put all the ingredients in a small bowl and mix together.

Cinnamon-Yoghurt Dressing

Indulge in this sweet and fat-free sensation.

Preparation time: 5 minutes

Yields: ½ cup

Ingredients:

¼ teaspoon of cinnamon

½ cup of no-fat plain yoghurt

Directions:

Whisk the ingredients in a bowl.

Berry-Balsamic Vinaigrette

This dressing is healthy, colorful, and of course, sweet.

Preparation time: 15 minutes

Yields: 2¼ cups

Ingredients:

2 cups of fresh or frozen strawberries, chopped and if frozen, thawed

2 tablespoons of balsamic vinegar

1/3 cup of olive oil

1 tablespoon of brown sugar

¼ teaspoon of kosher salt

¾ teaspoon of ground black pepper

Directions:

Blend all the ingredients in a blender until it is smooth.

Sweet Lime Dressing

Add this amazing citrus flavor to your salads.

Preparation time: 2 minutes

Yields: 1/8 cup

Ingredients:

2 tablespoons of granulated sugar

Juice of 1 lime

Directions:

Whisk the ingredients together in a small bowl.

Orange Vinaigrette

A mixture of spicy and sweet makes this dressing a hit.

Preparation time: 5 minutes

Yields: ¾ cup

Ingredients:

¼ cup of orange juice

1 green onion, finely diced

4 garlic cloves, crushed

3 tablespoons of red wine vinegar

1 teaspoon of orange peel, finely shredded

1 teaspoon of ground cinnamon

½ teaspoon of salt

¼ teaspoon of cayenne pepper

Directions:

1. Put all the ingredients except the olive oil in a bowl and combine thoroughly.

2. Add the oil slowly while whisking.

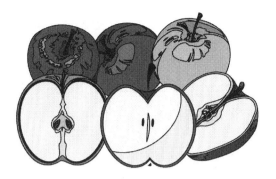

Peach-Honey Dressing

You can enjoy this sweet and yummy dressing with bread.

Preparation time: 2 minutes

Yields: ¾ cup

Ingredients:

1/3 cup of olive oil

3 tablespoons of peach nectar

3 tablespoons of honey

1 tablespoon of lemon juice

1 garlic clove

¼ teaspoon of salt

¼ teaspoon of ground black pepper

Directions:

1. Put all the ingredients except the olive oil in a food processor or blender and allow it run until it forms a smooth paste.

2. Add the oil slowly while the processor or blender is running. Stop when everything is thoroughly combined.

Honey-Citrus Salad Dressing
All the flavors of summer contained in one recipe.

Preparation time: 7 minutes

Yields: 1/3 cup

Ingredients:

2 tablespoons of honey

2 tablespoons of orange juice, freshly squeezed

½ tablespoon of lime juice, fresh

1 teaspoon of lime zest

1 teaspoon of orange zest

Directions:

In a small bowl, add all the ingredients and whisk until it is thoroughly combined.

Mango-Mint Salad Dressing
The perfect salad dressing!

Preparation time: 10 minutes

Yields: ¾ cup

Ingredients:

1 mango, peeled, pitted and chopped

1 tablespoon of fresh mint

¼ cup of rice vinegar

2 tablespoons of canola oil

2 green onions, diced

2 teaspoons of sesame oil, optional

A pinch of salt

Directions:

1. Put all the ingredients except the mint in a food processor or blender and allow it run until it forms a smooth paste.

2. Add the mint and continue pulsing until it is chopped

Poppy Seed-Raspberry Salad Dressing
Serve this over a salad with raspberry for a double dose of flavor.

Preparation time: 5 minutes

Yields: 2- 2½ cups

Ingredients:

8-10 raspberries

¾ cup of vegetable oil

½ cup of red wine vinegar

4-5 tablespoons of sugar

1 tablespoon of red onion, minced

2 teaspoons of poppy seeds

½ teaspoon of dried, powdered mustard

1 teaspoon of salt

Directions:

Add all the ingredients to a jar. Crush the raspberries a little before combining with the other ingredients.

Lime-Chile Sauce

A recipe that is packed with the flavors of Asia.

Preparation time: 10 minutes

Yields: ¾ cup

Ingredients:

¼ cup of lime juice

2 Thai chilies

¼ cup of honey

1 tablespoon of Thai fish sauce

1 tablespoon of fresh ginger, chopped

1 tablespoon of olive oil

2 garlic cloves, chopped

Directions:

Add all the ingredients to a food processor or blender and blend until it becomes very smooth.

Strawberry Vinaigrette

Entice your kids to eat their vegetables with this dressing.

Preparation time: 10 minutes

Yields: 1- 1½ cups

Ingredients:

½ pound of fresh strawberries

2 tablespoons of olive oil

2 tablespoons of honey

2 tablespoons of apple cider vinegar

¼ teaspoon of salt

¼ teaspoon of ground black pepper

Directions:

Add all the ingredients to a blender and blend until it becomes very smooth.

Lime-Honey Salad Dressing

Create a masterpiece with just four ingredients.

Preparation time: 5 minutes

Yields: 1 cup

Ingredients:

¼ cup of lime juice, freshly squeezed

¼ cup of honey

½ cup of plain yoghurt

1 teaspoon of lime peel, grated

Directions:

In a small bowl, add all the ingredients and whisk until it is thoroughly combined.

Fruit Salad Dressing

This delicious dressing is simple and easy to prepare.

Preparation time: 8 minutes

Cooking time: 2 minutes

Yields: 3 – 3½ cups

Ingredients:

2 cans (6-oz each) of pineapple juice

1 can (6-oz) of orange juice concentrate, thawed

¼ cup of lemon juice

¼ cup of honey

½-1 cup of sugar

3 tablespoons of all-purpose flour

Directions:

1. Mix all the ingredients together in a saucepan and leave to boil.

2. Allow to cook and stir for 2 minutes or until it becomes thick and bubbly

Lemon-Honey Salad Dressing

Add a tangy flavor to your fruit salad with this recipe.

Preparation time: 5 minutes

Yields: 1/3 cup

Ingredients:

2 tablespoons of honey

2 tablespoons of lemon juice

2 tablespoons of canola oil

1 teaspoon of Dijon mustard

¼ teaspoon of salt

1/8 teaspoon of ground white pepper

Directions:

1. Whisk together all the ingredients except the canola oil in a small bowl until it is well-combined.

2. While still whisking, drizzle in the oil slowly until the dressing emulsifies and thickens.

Honey Salad Dressing

Enhance the taste of your fruit salad with this decadent dressing.

Preparation time: 5 minutes

Yields: 1 cup

Ingredients:

1/3 cup of honey

¼ cup of canola oil

¼ cup of orange juice

1 ½ teaspoons of poppy seeds

½ teaspoon of fresh lemon juice

¼ teaspoon of prepared mustard

Juice of 1 lemon

¼ teaspoon of salt

Directions:

Add all the ingredients to a jar with a lid and shake until it is thoroughly mixed.

Vanilla Salad Dressing
Delight your taste buds with this thriller in vanilla.

Preparation time: 5 minutes

Yields: ¾ cup

Ingredients:

1 teaspoon of pure vanilla extract

½ cup of plain yoghurt

¼ cup of mayonnaise

1 teaspoon of honey

1 teaspoon of lemon juice

Freshly ground black pepper

¼ teaspoon of kosher salt

Directions:

In a small bowl, add all the ingredients except the pepper and whisk until it is thoroughly combined. Add pepper to season.

Fruit Juice Dressing
You can substitute the orange juice for any fruit juice of your choice.

Preparation time: 5 minutes

Yields: 2 1/3 cups

Ingredients:

½ cup of orange juice

½ cup of balsamic vinegar

1 cup of olive oil

1 tablespoon of fruit jam

1 tablespoon of mustard

A clove of garlic

Pepper

Directions:

Combine all the ingredients in a bowl.

Healthy Salad Dressing

This goes along with your fruit salads perfectly.

Preparation time: 5 minutes

Yields: 1 cup

Ingredients:

2/3 cup of baking blend

½ cup of water

2 tablespoons of raw vinegar

2 tablespoons of extra-virgin olive oil

2 teaspoons of lemon juice

Directions:

Add all the ingredients to a shaker or jar and shake until it mixes
thoroughly.

Yoghurt Dressing

You can use it for your salads or as a dipping sauce for your fruits.

Preparation time: 10 minutes

Yields: 2 – 2½ cups

Ingredients:

½ cup of vanilla yoghurt

½ cup of fat-free sour cream

½ cup of apple juice

1 package (8-ounce) fat-free cream cheese

Directions:

Add all the ingredients to a food processor or blender and blend until it becomes very smooth.

Vanilla-Honey Dressing

A delicious combination of vanilla, honey and yoghurt.

Preparation time: 5 minutes

Yields: 2 1/8 cups

Ingredients:

½ teaspoon of pure vanilla extract

2 tablespoons of honey

2 cups of plain yoghurt

Directions:

Whisk the ingredients together in a bowl.

Lemon-Honey Salad Dressing

Bring out the flavors of your fruit salads with this sweet and tart dressing.

Preparation time: 5 minutes

Cooking time: 7 minutes

Yields: ½ cup

Ingredients:

¼ cup of lemon juice, freshly squeezed

Zest of 3 lemons

3 tablespoons of honey

3 tablespoons of water

Directions:

1. In a small saucepan, mix all the ingredients and allow to boil.

2. Reduce the heat and leave to simmer for 3-5 minutes. Remove from heat and leave to cool

Ginger Lime Honey Salad Dressing
Three of our favorite ingredients combine to mix this yummy treat.

Preparation time: 5 minutes

Yields: ¾ cup

Ingredients:

2 tablespoons of fresh ginger, finely grated

Juice and zest of 1 lime

½ cup of honey

2 teaspoon of poppy seed

Directions:

Whisk the ingredients together in a bowl.

Mint-Lime Dressing
Infuse the subtle flavor of mint into your fruit salad.

Preparation time: 5 minutes

Cooking time: 10 minutes

Yields: ¾ - 1 cup

Ingredients:

½ cup of packed mint leaves

Zest of 1 lime

½ cup of sugar

½ cup of water

Directions:

1. In a small pan, boil the water and sugar. Ensure that the sugar is dissolved.

2. Turn off heat; add the mint and lime zest to the pan and leave to steep for 15 minutes.

Mint-Watermelon Salad Dressing

A unique dressing made with only two ingredients.

Preparation time: 5 minutes

Yields: ½ - ¾ cup

Ingredients:

15-20 mint leaves

1 cup of watermelon chunks

Directions:

Add all the ingredients to a blender and blend until the mint is chopped and the watermelon becomes liquid.

Poppy Seed Dressing

Creamy, tangy and delicious.

Preparation time: 5 minutes

Yields: ½ cup

Ingredients:

¼ cup of sour cream

2 tablespoons of lemon juice

2 tablespoons of maple syrup

1 teaspoon of lemon zest

1 teaspoon of poppy seeds

Salt

Directions:

Whisk all the ingredients except the salt in a bowl and then season with salt.

Orange Pineapple Dressing

Make this exotic dressing with ingredients from your kitchen.

Preparation time: 15 minutes

Yields: 2 cups

Ingredients:

1 can (11-oz) of mandarin oranges

½ cup of fresh pineapple chunks

2 tablespoons of lime or lemon juice, fresh

2 tablespoons of chopped fresh parsley

2 tablespoons of honey

1 tablespoon of vegetable oil

¼ teaspoon of salt

¼ teaspoon of black pepper

Directions:

Add all the ingredients to a food processor or blender and blend until it becomes very smooth.

NEW/POPULAR SALAD DRESSINGS

Lime Herb Salad Dressing

Savor the mix of your favorite herbs with the tangy flavor of lime.

Preparation time: 10 minutes

Yields: 1½ - 2 cups

Ingredients:

¼ cup of lime juice, freshly squeezed

¼ cup of olive oil

½ cup of packed fresh mint leaves

½ cup of packed arugula

½ cup of vegetable oil

1 jalapeno or Serrano chili, chopped and seeded

½ teaspoon of sugar

½ teaspoon of lime zest, finely grated

Kosher salt

Freshly ground black pepper

Directions:

Put all the ingredients except the salt and pepper in a blender. Puree until it become smooth. Add salt and pepper to season.

Tahini-Turmeric Salad Dressing

This dressing's yellow color contrasts beautifully with your salads.

Preparation time: 5 minutes

Yields: ½ - ¾ cup

Ingredients:

¼ cup of tahini

½ teaspoon of ground turmeric

3 tablespoons of lemon juice, freshly squeezed

2 tablespoons of olive oil

¼ teaspoon of cayenne pepper

Kosher salt

Freshly ground black pepper

Directions:

Put all the ingredients except the salt and pepper in a bowl and whisk until it becomes smooth. Add salt and pepper to season.

Sesame-Miso Dressing

Prepare this popular Japanese dressing with ingredients from your kitchen.

Preparation time: 5 minutes

Yields: 1½ cups

Ingredients:

½ teaspoon of sesame oil

½ cup of white miso paste

¼ cup of sugar

¼ cup of water, plus 1 tablespoon

3 tablespoons of rice wine vinegar

2 tablespoons of peanut oil

2 teaspoons of peanut oil

¼ teaspoon of kosher salt

Directions:

1. Put all the ingredients except the peanut and sesame oils in a bowl and whisk until it becomes smooth.

2. Add the oils slowly while whisking until the mixture becomes creamy.

Coffee Vinaigrette

Pep up your salads with the active flavors of coffee.

Preparation time: 12 minutes

Yields: 1/3 cup

Ingredients:

1 teaspoon of coffee

½ cup of extra-virgin olive oil

1 teaspoon of sugar

¼ cup of sherry wine vinegar

½ teaspoon of salt

½ teaspoon of freshly ground black pepper

Directions:

1. Put all the ingredients except the olive oil in a bowl and whisk until it becomes smooth.

2. Add the oil slowly while whisking until it is thoroughly combined

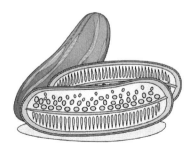

Shallot Vinaigrette

This easy recipe comes together in just five minutes.

Preparation time: 25 minutes

Yields: ¾ cup

Ingredients:

1 shallot, finely diced

1/3 cup of olive oil

2 tablespoons of lemon juice, freshly squeezed

1 tablespoon of rice vinegar

Kosher salt

Freshly ground black pepper

Directions:

1. Add the shallot, lemon juice and vinegar in a jar and mix together.

2. Add salt and pepper to season and allow it to stand for 20 minutes.

3. Pour in the olive oil, close the jar and shake thoroughly to combine well.

Easy Asian Dressing

We promise that this recipe is as easy as it sounds.

Preparation time: 5 minutes

Yields: 1/3 cup

Ingredients:

½ cup of olive oil

½ small-sized clove of garlic, finely grated

2 teaspoons of unseasoned rice vinegar

½ teaspoon of sesame oil

1 tablespoon of low-sodium soy sauce

Kosher salt

Freshly ground black pepper

Directions:

1. Put garlic, vinegar and soy sauce in a bowl and whisk together.

2. Drizzle in the olive oil and then the sesame oil slowly while whisking until it is thoroughly combined.

3. Add salt and pepper to season.

Sesame-Soy Salad Dressing

You can also eat this dressing with noodles.

Preparation time: 5 minutes

Yields: 1 cup

Ingredients:

¼ cup of toasted sesame oil

2 tablespoons of soy sauce

4 scallions, diced

1/3 cup of unseasoned rice vinegar

1 tablespoon of ginger, finely grated

1 tablespoon of tahini

1 tablespoon of lime juice, freshly squeezed

Kosher salt

Freshly ground black pepper

Directions:

1. In a small bowl, whisk together all the ingredients except the salt and pepper.

2. Add salt and pepper to season.

Lemon-Soy Dressing

Enjoy this light and lemony dressing with your green salads.

Preparation time: 5 minutes

Yields: 1½ cups

Ingredients:

2/3 cup of lemon juice

1 tablespoon of finely grated lemon peel

2/3 cup of soy sauce

¼ teaspoon of garlic powder

4 ½ teaspoons of sugar

Directions:

Add all the ingredients to a jar with a lid and shake until it is thoroughly mixed and the sugar is dissolved.

Lime-Chili Dressing

Add some kick to your salads with this recipe.

Preparation time: 5 minutes

Yields: ½ cup

Ingredients:

¼ cup of lime juice, freshly squeezed

1 tablespoon of chili oil

2 tablespoons of soy sauce

1 teaspoon of crushed garlic

1 tablespoon of golden brown sugar

Directions:

1. In a medium-sized bowl, whisk together all the ingredients.

2. Add pepper to season.

Miso-Berry Dressing

This unique recipe has an intense flavor that combines ideally with your salads.

Preparation time: 10 minutes

Yields: 1 cup

Ingredients:

1 tablespoon of white miso

1 tablespoon of blackberry jam

¼ cup of water

¼ cup of apple cider vinegar

1 tablespoon of hemp seeds

¼ cup of tamari

1 tablespoon of dried onion flakes

1 garlic clove

½ teaspoon of black pepper

Directions:

Put all the ingredients in a blender and blend until it is totally smooth.

Pineapple Salad Dressing

Creamy, light and low in calories.

Preparation time: 7 minutes

Yields: 1- 1¼ cup

Ingredients:

½ cup of unsweetened pineapple juice

2 tablespoons of Dijon mustard

2 teaspoons of fresh ginger, grated

½ cup of mayonnaise

½ tablespoon of honey

Directions:

In a bowl, whisk together all the ingredients.

Russian Salad Dressing

Mayonnaise and tomato ketchup come together to create this creamy and spicy dressing.

Preparation time: 10 minutes

Yields: 1½ cups

Ingredients:

1 cup of mayonnaise

¼ cup of ketchup

1 tablespoon of finely diced onion

4 teaspoons of regular bottled horseradish

1 teaspoon of Worcestershire sauce

1 teaspoon of hot sauce

¼ teaspoon of sweet paprika

Directions:

1. Using a big heavy knife or mortar and pestle, mash the onion into a paste.

2. In a small bowl mix the onion paste with the mayo, ketchup, horseradish, Worcestershire sauce, hot sauce and paprika.

3. Taste and season with salt if needed.

Benihana Ginger Salad Dressing

Douse your salads in this sweet and tangy ginger dressing.

Preparation time: 10 minutes

Yields: 1½ - 2 cups

Ingredients:

2 tablespoons of crushed fresh ginger

½ cup of crushed onion

2 teaspoons of lemon juice

½ cup of peanut oil

4 teaspoons of soy sauce

1/3 cup of rice vinegar

½ teaspoon of crushed garlic

2 tablespoons of crushed celery

2 tablespoons of water

2 tablespoons of ketchup

2 teaspoons of granulated sugar

½ teaspoon of salt

¼ teaspoon of ground black pepper

Directions:

Put all the ingredients in a blender and blend until it is smooth.

Parmesan Pepper Dressing

Complement your favorite salad with this dressing.

Preparation time: 5 minutes

Yields: 1¾ - 2 cups

Ingredients:

¼ cup of parmesan cheese, freshly grated

1 cup of mayonnaise

1 tablespoon of cracked pepper

1 tablespoon of dill weed

2 tablespoons of red wine vinegar

¼ cup of milk

1 teaspoon of onion powder

½ tablespoon of paprika

¼ teaspoon of lemon juice

½ tablespoon of garlic salt

A dash of Worcestershire sauce

A dash of hot pepper sauce, optional

Directions:

Whisk together all the ingredients in a medium-sized bowl.

Roasted Pepper Vinaigrette

You can either roast your own peppers or purchase them at the store.

Preparation time: 5 minutes

Yields: 1 cup

Ingredients:

¼ cup of extra-virgin olive oil

1 cup of jarred roasted peppers, washed and rinsed

3 tablespoons of sherry vinegar

1 teaspoon of smoked paprika

2 garlic cloves

¼ teaspoon of salt

¼ teaspoon of freshly ground pepper

Directions:

Add all the ingredients to a food processor or blender and blend until it becomes very smooth.

Peppercorn Salad Dressing

This recipe can stay for up to two weeks.

Preparation time: 5 minutes

Yields: 2½ - 3 cups

Ingredients:

2 teaspoons of roughly ground pepper

¼ cup of milk

1 cup of mayonnaise

3 tablespoons of lemon juice

1 cup (8-oz) sour cream

½ teaspoon of onion powder

1/3 cup of Parmesan cheese, grated

½ teaspoon of garlic salt

Directions:

Whisk all the ingredients together in a small bowl.

Sweet Onion Dressing
Has a lemony taste that is just refreshing.

Preparation time: 5 minutes

Yields: 1 ½cups

Ingredients:

2 teaspoons of chopped sweet onion

½ cup of white sugar

1 teaspoon of Dijon mustard

2/3 cup of vegetable oil

½ cup of lemon juice, freshly squeezed

1 tablespoon of poppy seeds

½ teaspoon of salt

Directions:

Add all the ingredients to a food processor or blender and blend until it becomes very smooth.

Cranberry Dressing
Looks pretty and tastes delicious.

Preparation time: 10 minutes

Yields: 2 – 2½ cups

Ingredients:

1 cup of cranberries

1 cup of vegetable oil

½ cup of vinegar

2/3 cup of sugar

1 teaspoon of onion, grated

1 teaspoon of ground mustard

1 teaspoon of salt

Directions:

1. Put all the ingredients except the vegetable oil in a blender and allow it run until it forms a smooth paste.

2. Drizzle in the oil slowly while the processor is running.

Apricot-Orange Salad Dressing
Its citrusy flavor adds an instant appeal to all salads.

Preparation time: 5 minutes

Yields: ¾ cup

Ingredients:

¼ cup of apricot preservatives

2 tablespoons of canola oil

2 tablespoons of orange juice

1 tablespoon of water

2 tablespoons of rice vinegar

1/8 teaspoon of salt

A dash of pepper

Directions:

Add all the ingredients to a jar with a lid and shake until it is thoroughly mixed.

Cilantro Dressing
This can be served over greens or potatoes.

Preparation time: 5 minutes

Yields: ¾ cup

Ingredients:

½ cup of fresh cilantro leaves

¼ cup of no-fat mayonnaise

¼ cup of buttermilk

1/8 teaspoon of sugar

3-6 drops of hot pepper sauce

¼ teaspoon of garlic powder

¼ teaspoon of salt

Directions:

Add all the ingredients to a blender and blend until it becomes very smooth.

Mustard Salad Dressing

Enjoy this simple dressing with your green salads.

Preparation time: 2 minutes

Yields: 1/5 cup

Ingredients:

3 tablespoons of Dijon mustard

¼ teaspoon of sugar

1 teaspoon of white wine vinegar

Directions:

Whisk together the ingredients in a bowl.

Herby Cucumber Dressing

Puree your cucumber to make this creamy and healthy dressing.

Preparation time: 5 minutes

Yields: 1¼ -1¾ cups

Ingredients:

1 small-sized cucumber, peeled, seeded and diced

1 teaspoon of Dijon mustard

¼ cup of extra-virgin olive oil

2 tablespoons of chopped fresh parsley

1 teaspoon of sugar

2 tablespoons of red wine vinegar

1 teaspoon of prepared horseradish

2 tablespoons of fresh chives

1 tablespoon of low-fat or fat-free plain yoghurt

½ teaspoon of salt

Directions:

Add all the ingredients to a blender and blend until it becomes very smooth.

Sour Cream Dressing

Add this sweet and gorgeous recipe to any of your boring salads.

Preparation time: 7 minutes

Yields: 1¼ cup

Ingredients:

1 cup of sour cream

1 tablespoon of lemon juice

1/8 teaspoon of paprika

2 tablespoons of vinegar

1 teaspoon of sugar

1 teaspoon of salt

Directions:

1. In a bowl, combine all the ingredients except the sour cream and stir until the sugar and salt dissolves.

2. Whisk in the sour cream and mix until it is smooth.

Worcestershire Dressing

Make your own tangy dressing with basic ingredients.

Preparation time: 5 minutes

Yields: 2/5 cup

Ingredients:

2 tablespoons of Worcestershire sauce

2 tablespoons of lemon juice

2 tablespoons white wine vinegar

1 tablespoon of olive oil

Directions:

Add all the ingredients to a jar or bowl and shake or whisk together.

Thousand Island Dressing
Taste better than the version sold in stores and is a lot less expensive!

Preparation time: 5 minutes

Yields: ¾ cup

Ingredients:

2 tablespoons of sweet pickle relish

½ cup of mayonnaise

2 teaspoons of finely chopped onion

2 tablespoons of ketchup

1 teaspoon of white vinegar

¼ teaspoon of finely crushed garlic

2-3 dashes of Tabasco sauce

1/8 teaspoon of salt

Directions:

Whisk together all the ingredients in a small bowl.

Garlic Dressing
This thick salad dressing will add flavor to any salad.

Preparation time: 5 minutes

Yields: 1½ cups

Ingredients:

3 cloves of garlic

1 cup of olive oil

2 teaspoons of dried herbs

½ cup of fresh lemon juice

½ teaspoon of sea salt

Directions:

Add all the ingredients to a blender and blend until it becomes very smooth.

German Salad Dressing

Prepare this easy salad dressing the traditional German way.

Preparation time: 5 minutes

Yields: ¾ cup

Ingredients:

2 tablespoons of vinegar

½ cup of milk

2 tablespoons of honey or sugar

Directions:

Whisk all the ingredients together.

Rosewater Vinaigrette

Add a flavorful fragrance to your salads with this recipe.

Preparation time: 5 minutes

Yields: ½ cup

Ingredients:

¼ cup of olive oil

1 tablespoon of rosewater

1 tablespoon of water

1 tablespoon of lime or orange juice

2 tbsp white wine vinegar

A pinch of salt

A pinch of pepper

A pinch of cardamom spice

Directions:

1. Add all the ingredients except the olive oil to a jar and shake thoroughly.

2. Add in the oil and continue shaking until it is well-combined.

Homemade Salad Dressing

Host your guests with this special homemade dressing

Preparation time: 5 minutes

Yields: 1½ cup

Ingredients:

½ cup of buttermilk

¼ cup of parmesan cheese, grated

¾ cup of cottage cheese

1 scallion, diced

½ teaspoon of Italian seasoning

¼ teaspoon of black pepper

Directions:

Add all the ingredients to a food processor or blender and blend until it becomes very smooth.

Herb Dressing

This creamy dressing is a delicious addition to your salads.

Preparation time: 5 minutes

Yields: ¾ cup

Ingredients:

2 tablespoons of fresh herbs, chopped

¼ cup of mayonnaise

½ cup of buttermilk

½ teaspoon of kosher salt

¼ teaspoon of black pepper

Directions:

Add all the ingredients to a small bowl and whisk together to combine.

Garlic-Lemon Salad Dressing

The flavors in this dressing make it an amazing addition to any type of salad.

Preparation time: 5 minutes

Yields: 3/5 cup

Ingredients:

1 small-sized garlic clove, minced

3 tablespoons of lemon juice, freshly squeezed

1/3 cup of olive oil

¼ teaspoon of kosher salt

¼ teaspoon of pepper

Directions:

Add all the ingredients to a small bowl and whisk together to combine.

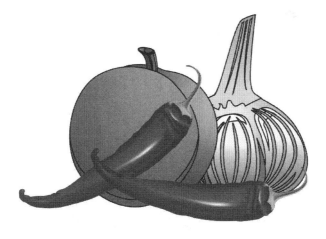

Parmesan Salad Dressing

Prepare this tasty and creamy dressing with just a few ingredients.

Preparation time: 5 minutes

Yields: 1½ cup

Ingredients:

½ cup of parmesan, grated

½ cup of olive oil

¼ cup of sour cream

2 tablespoons of water

2 tablespoons white wine vinegar

¼ teaspoon of kosher salt

¼ teaspoon of black pepper

Directions:

Add all the ingredients to a small bowl and whisk together to combine.

Blue Cheese Salad Dressing

If you are having a hard time eating your salads, then you should try this amazing dressing.

Preparation time: 5 minutes

Yields: 1- 1¼ cup

Ingredients:

4 ounces of blue cheese, crumbled

½ cup of buttermilk

¼ cup of sour cream

¼ teaspoon of black pepper

Directions:

1. Add the buttermilk, sour cream and pepper to a small bowl and whisk together to combine.

2. Fold the blue cheese into the mixture.

Blueberry Salad Dressing

Make your own homemade blueberry dressing.

Preparation time: 5 minutes

Yields: ½ - ¾ cup

Ingredients:

½ cup of fresh or frozen blueberries, thawed and divided

2 tablespoons of orange marmalade

¼ cup of vegetable oil

2 teaspoons of lemon juice

1 teaspoon of Dijon mustard

¼ teaspoon of salt

Directions:

Add all the ingredients to a blender and blend until it becomes very smooth.

Dijon Salad Dressing
Simple to prepare and of course, packed with flavors.

Preparation time: 5 minutes

Yields: 1½ cups

Ingredients:

1 tablespoon of Dijon mustard

½ cup of cider vinegar

1 tablespoon of onion, grated

1 cup of vegetable oil

1 tablespoon of sugar

¾ teaspoon of salt

Directions

Add all the ingredients to a medium bowl and whisk together to combine.

Ranch Salad Dressing

You will never buy another at the store after making this.

Preparation time: 5 minutes

Yields: 1¼ cup

Ingredients:

1 teaspoon of white vinegar

1 cup of mayonnaise

1 clove of garlic, crushed

¼ cup of buttermilk

1 teaspoon of crushed fresh dill

1/8 teaspoon of sugar

1/8 teaspoon of salt

1/8 teaspoon of black pepper

Directions:

Add all the ingredients to a medium bowl and whisk together to combine.

Pumpkin Salad Dressing

Get in tune with the fall season with this seasonal dressing

Preparation time: 5 minutes

Yields: 1 cup

Ingredients:

1 tablespoon of apple cider vinegar

1/3 cup of pumpkin

2 tablespoons of maple syrup

½ cup of plain Greek yoghurt

1 tablespoon of canola oil

¼ teaspoon of ground cinnamon

1/8 teaspoon of salt

Directions:

Add all the ingredients to a medium bowl and whisk together to combine.

Classic Italian Dressing
The much loved traditional Italian dressing.

Preparation time: 5 minutes

Yields: 1¼ cup

Ingredients:

1/3 cup of apple cider vinegar

¾ cup of canola oil

¼ teaspoon of dry mustard

2 teaspoons of granulated splenda

1 teaspoon of Italian seasoning

½ teaspoon of celery salt

¼ teaspoon of ground red pepper

Directions:

Add all the ingredients to a jar with a lid and shake until it is thoroughly mixed.

Traditional Vinaigrette

Make this little recipe for that special occasion.

Preparation time: 2 minutes

Yields: ¾ cup

Ingredients:

4 tablespoons of lemon juice, freshly squeezed

½ cup of olive oil

1 teaspoon of Dijon mustard

¼ teaspoon of salt

¼ teaspoon of fresh ground black pepper

Directions:

Add all the ingredients to a bowl and whisk together to combine.

Green Goddess Salad Dressing

Prepared with herbs that can be found in your garden

Preparation time: 10 minutes

Yields: 2 cups

Ingredients:

½ cup of chopped parsley

¾ cup of sour cream

¾ cup of mayonnaise

¼ cup of diced tarragon

2 teaspoons of anchovy paste

2 tablespoon of lemon juice

3 tablespoons of chopped chives

Salt

Black pepper

Directions:

Add all the ingredients to a food processor or blender and blend until it becomes very smooth.

Buttermilk Ranch Salad Dressing

Switch up the taste of your ranch salad with the addition of buttermilk.

Preparation time: 5 minutes

Yields: 1½ - 1¾ cups

Ingredients:

1 teaspoon of lemon juice

1 teaspoon of chopped fresh chives

1 cup of buttermilk

1 teaspoon of chopped fresh dill

1 tablespoon of chopped fresh parsley

½ cup of mayonnaise

¼ teaspoon of mustard powder

1/8 teaspoon of paprika

½ teaspoon of salt

1/8 teaspoon of black pepper

Directions:

1. Combine the mayo and buttermilk in a medium-sized bowl.

2. Add in the remaining ingredients.

Coconut Cream Salad Dressing

Complement your plain salads with this amazing dressing.

Preparation time: 5 minutes

Yields: 1¼ cup

Ingredients:

1 can (8.5-oz) of cream of coconut

1 package (0.7-oz) of dry Italian salad dressing mix

¼ cup of cider vinegar

Directions:

Add all the ingredients to a bowl and whisk together to combine.

Creamy Dressing
Add more flavor to your salads with this recipe

Preparation time: 5 minutes

Yields: 1/6 cup

Ingredients:

1 ½ tablespoons of mayonnaise

1 tablespoon of champagne vinegar

1 teaspoon of Dijon mustard

A pinch of sugar

A pinch of salt

Fresh pepper

Directions:

1. Add all the ingredients except the vinegar to a bowl and whisk together to combine.

2. Add in the vinegar and continue whisking until the mixture is smooth.

Creamy Blue Cheese Salad Dressing
Add mayonnaise to this dressing to make it extra creamy than the normal version.

Preparation time: 8 minutes

Yields: 1¼ cup

Ingredients:

2 tablespoons of mayonnaise

4 ounces of blue cheese, crumbled

2 tablespoons of lemon juice

¼ cup of buttermilk

¼ cup of sour cream

Salt

Pepper

Directions:

1. Mash the sour cream and cheese in a small bowl until it forms a paste.

2. Add the mayonnaise, lemon juice, and buttermilk. Stir to combine.

3. Add salt and pepper to season.

Caesar Salad Dressing
Make your own original salad dressing.

Preparation time: 15 minutes

Yields: 1- 1½ cups

Ingredients:

½ cup of vegetable oil

2 tablespoons of lemon juice, freshly squeezed

6 anchovy fillets

3 tablespoons of parmesan, finely grated

2 large egg yolks

1 small clove of garlic

2 tablespoons of olive oil

¾ teaspoon of Dijon mustard

Kosher salt

Freshly ground black pepper

Directions:

1. Chop the anchovies, garlic, and combine with a pinch of salt. Mash everything together into a paste with the side of a knife blade and put in a medium-sized bowl.

2. Whisk in the egg yolks, lemon juice and mustard.

3. Slowly drizzle in the olive oil followed by the vegetable oil until it looks glossy and thickens.

4. While still whisking, add the parmesan and season with salt and pepper.

Egg-Free Caesar Salad Dressing

If you are not a fan of eggs, this recipe is perfect for you.

Preparation time: 10 minutes

Yields: 1½ - 2 cups

Ingredients:

1 tablespoon of Dijon mustard

3 garlic cloves, diced

5 anchovy fillets

¼ cup of lemon juice

½ cup of extra-virgin olive oil

2 tablespoons of red wine vinegar or sherry

½ cup of grated parmesan cheese

1 teaspoon of freshly ground black pepper

Directions:

1. Mash the garlic, anchovy fillets, and pepper with a mortar and pestle.

2. Whisk in the mustard, lemon juice, and vinegar.

3. Drizzle in the oil slowly while whisking until it becomes emulsified.

4. Add the parmesan and adjust taste.

Asian Ginger Salad Dressing
Prepare your own delicious Asian cuisine with this recipe.

Preparation time: 5 minutes

Yields: 2 – 2¼ cups

Ingredients:

½ cup of soy sauce

¾ cup of olive oil

¼ cup of water

1/3 cup of rice vinegar

3 cloves of garlic, crushed

3 tablespoons of warm honey

2 tablespoons of crushed ginger

Directions:

Add all the ingredients to a jar with a lid and shake until it is thoroughly mixed.

Lemon Yoghurt Honey Dressing
Jazz up your salads with this light and creamy dressing.

Preparation time: 5 minutes

Yields: 1 1/3 cup

Ingredients:

1 tablespoon of lemon juice

1 cup of yoghurt

2 tablespoons of honey, warm

2 tablespoons of apple cider vinegar

Salt

Freshly ground black pepper

Directions:

1. Add the honey, yoghurt, and vinegar to a jar and shake.

2. Pour in the lemon juice and thoroughly combine.

3. Season with salt and pepper

VINAIGRETTES

Red Wine Vinaigrettes

An excellent and rich vinaigrette.

Preparation time: 5 minutes

Yields: ½ cup

Ingredients:

1/3 cup of olive oil

3 tablespoons of red wine vinegar

1 teaspoon of Dijon mustard

1 teaspoon of honey

½ teaspoon of salt

¼ teaspoon of black pepper

Directions:

Put all the ingredients in a small bowl and mix together.

Simple Vinaigrette

An amazing vinaigrette that is totally easy to prepare.

Preparation time: 5 minutes

Yields: 4/5 cup

Ingredients:

¼ cup of lemon juice, freshly squeezed

1 small-sized shallot, crushed

1 teaspoon of honey

½ cup of extra-virgin olive oil

½ teaspoon of salt

¼ teaspoon of freshly ground black pepper

Directions:

1. Put the lemon juice, shallot and honey in a small bowl and whisk together.

2. Add the oil slowly while whisking until it becomes emulsified.

3. Season with salt and pepper.

Dijon-Balsamic Vinaigrette

What could be better than this mouth-watering combination of Dijon and balsamic vinegar?

Preparation time: 5 minutes

Yields: 2/3 cup

Ingredients:

½ cup of olive oil

2 teaspoons of Dijon mustard

3 tablespoons of balsamic vinegar

½ teaspoon of salt

¼ teaspoon of pepper

Directions:

Add all the ingredients to a small jar or bowl. Shake or whisk together.

White Wine Vinaigrette

Obviously, if there is a red wine vinaigrette, there should also be a recipe for white wine vinaigrette.

Preparation time: 5 minutes

Yields: 1 1/3 cups

Ingredients:

1/3 cup of white wine

¼ cup of fresh lemon juice

1 teaspoon of honey

¼ teaspoon of black pepper

¼ teaspoon of salt

¾ cup of extra-virgin olive oil

Directions:

1. Add the wine, lemon juice, honey, salt and pepper to a medium-sized bowl and whisk together.

2. While you are whisking, add the oil slowly until it emulsifies.

Shallot And Lemon Vinaigrette

You will love the tart and refreshing taste of this dressing.

Preparation time: 5 minutes

Yields: ½ cup

Ingredients:

¼ cup of olive oil

¼ cup of lemon juice, freshly squeezed

1 shallot, finely diced

2 teaspoons of honey

¼ teaspoon of black pepper

½ teaspoon of salt

Directions:

Whisk all the ingredients together in a small bowl.

Roasted Lemon Vinaigrette

Try this recipe if you are feeling a little adventurous in the kitchen.

Preparation time: 10 minutes

Cooking time: 45 minutes

Yields: 2/3 cup

Ingredients:

2 lemons

1 tablespoon of honey

1 teaspoon of olive oil

½ teaspoon of kosher salt

3 tablespoons of extra-virgin olive oil

Directions:

1. Preheat the oven to 400F.

2. Divide the lemons crosswise and remove its seeds.

3. Place the divided lemons in a baking dish and drizzle olive oil on it.

4. Place the cut-side of the lemon down and roast for 25-45 minutes until it is soft and a little golden.

5. Remove from oven, squeeze the lemon juice and pulp into a small jar or bowl. Add the honey and salt.

6. Slowly add the extra-virgin olive oil while whisking.

Easy Vinaigrette

Just throw all the ingredients in a bowl, it's that simple.

Preparation time: 5 minutes

Yields: ¼ cup

Ingredients:

1 teaspoon of Dijon mustard

3 tablespoons of olive oil

1 tablespoon of red wine vinegar

½ small-sized shallot, finely diced

½ teaspoon of salt

1/8 teaspoon of black pepper

Directions:

Whisk all the ingredients together in a small bowl.

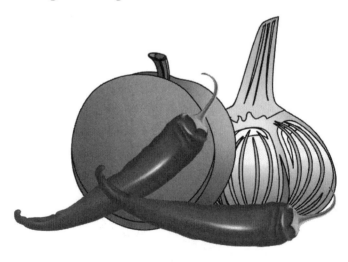

Dijon-Garlic Vinaigrette

This recipe can be eaten with everything!

Preparation time: 5 minutes

Yields: 1¾ cup

Ingredients:

¼ cup of Dijon mustard

½ cup of extra-virgin olive oil

½ cup of red wine vinegar

½ cup of lemon juice

4 small-sized cloves of garlic, crushed

½ teaspoon of salt

Freshly ground pepper

Directions:

1. Add all the ingredients except the salt and pepper in a medium bowl and whisk until its texture is smooth.

2. Add salt and pepper to season.

Mustard-Honey Vinaigrette

This recipe can also be used as a dipping sauce.

Preparation time: 5 minutes

Yields: 1 cup

Ingredients:

1 garlic clove, crushed

1 ½ teaspoons of Dijon mustard

1 tablespoon of white wine vinegar

1 cup of extra-virgin olive oil

½ teaspoon of honey

1/8 teaspoon of salt

Freshly ground black pepper

Directions:

1. In a small bowl, whisk together the garlic, mustard, vinegar, honey, salt and pepper.

2. While still whisking, add in the oil slowly.

Sesame Tamari Vinaigrette

This recipe goes perfectly with Asian food.

Preparation time: 5 minutes

Yields: 3/5 cup

Ingredients:

¼ cup of orange juice

¼ cup of rice vinegar

2 tablespoons of low-sodium tamari

1 tablespoon of honey

1 teaspoon of fresh ginger, finely grated

Directions:

In a small bowl, add the ingredients and whisk together. Only stop when the honey is well-mixed with the other ingredients.

Maple-Balsamic Vinaigrette

A sweet and sour recipe for your salads.

Preparation time: 5 minutes

Yields: 1/3 cup

Ingredients:

2 tablespoons of extra-virgin olive oil

2 teaspoons of maple syrup

2 tablespoons of balsamic vinegar

2 teaspoons of whole grain mustard

Salt

Freshly ground pepper

Directions:

1. In a small bowl, whisk together the vinegar, maple syrup and mustard until it is thoroughly blended.

2. Add salt and pepper to season

Apple Cider Vinaigrette
This recipe is fast and convenient.

Preparation time: 5 minutes

Yields: 1¼ cup

Ingredients:

¾ cup of olive oil

¼ cup of apple cider vinegar

2 tablespoons of honey

2 tablespoons of water

1 ½ teaspoons of salt

¼ teaspoon of pepper

Directions:

1. In a blender, mix together the vinegar, water, honey, salt and pepper.

2. Drizzle the oil into the blender until it mixes well with the other ingredients.

Lemon Vinaigrette

The tangy flavor of the lemon makes this a requirement for all salads.

Preparation time: 5 minutes

Yields: 1 cup

Ingredients:

¼ cup of red wine vinegar

1 garlic clove, finely crushed

2 tablespoons of Dijon mustard

1 tablespoon of honey

½ cup of extra-virgin olive oil

1 tablespoon of fresh oregano, minced

Zest and juice from 1 lemon

1 teaspoon of salt

¼ teaspoon of black pepper

Directions:

Add all the ingredients to a jar with a lid and shake until it is thoroughly mixed.

Balsamic Vinaigrette

Quick, easy and of course, tasty.

Preparation time: 5 minutes

Yields: 1 1/8 cup

Ingredients:

½ cup of balsamic vinegar

½ cup of extra-virgin olive oil

2 teaspoons of Dijon mustard

1 garlic clove, finely crushed

1 tablespoon of honey

1 teaspoon of salt

¼ teaspoon of black pepper

Directions:

Add all the ingredients to a jar with a lid and shake until it is thoroughly mixed.

Avocado Vinaigrette

You cannot go wrong with this creamy and healthy recipe.

Preparation time: 5 minutes

Yields: 1½ cup

Ingredients:

1 ripe avocado

Juice from 1 lemon

¾ cup of extra-virgin olive oil

¼ cup of white wine vinegar

Salt

Pepper

Directions:

1. Put all the ingredients except the olive oil in a food processor and allow it run until it becomes totally smooth and creamy.

2. Add the oil slowly while the processor is running on low stream. Stop when everything is thoroughly combined.

Clementine Vinaigrette

The combination of honey, clementine, vinegar, and mustard gives this recipe an absolutely delicious taste.

Preparation time: 5 minutes

Yields: 1½ - 1¾ cup

Ingredients:

Juice and zest from 2 clementines

2 tablespoons of apple cider vinegar

1 tablespoon of honey

1 cup of olive oil

1 teaspoon of Dijon mustard

½ teaspoon of garlic powder

Salt

Pepper

Directions:

Add all the ingredients to a jar with a lid and shake until it is thoroughly mixed.

Sesame-Lemon Vinaigrette

A creamy and delicious Asian-inspired recipe.

Preparation time: 5 minutes

Yields: ¼ cup

Ingredients:

1 tablespoon of tahini

1 tablespoon of rice wine vinegar

1 tablespoon of lemon juice

1 teaspoon of sesame oil

1 teaspoon of honey

1 garlic clove, minced

Pinch of red pepper flakes

¼ teaspoon of oregano

¼ teaspoon of salt

¼ teaspoon of black pepper

Directions:

Add all the ingredients to a jar with a lid and shake until the tahini is thoroughly mixed with the other ingredients.

Poppy Seed-Lemon Vinaigrette

This recipe adds a wonderful touch to your salads.

Preparation time: 5 minutes

Yields: ¾ cup

Ingredients:

¼ cup of olive oil

2 tbsp white wine vinegar

2 tsp Dijon mustard

1 teaspoon of poppy seeds

1 tsp honey

½ tsp garlic powder

Zest and juice of 1 lemon

Salt

Pepper

Directions:

Add all the ingredients to a jar with a lid and shake until it is thoroughly mixed.

Fresh Vinaigrette

Perfect for a green salad.

Preparation time: 5 minutes

Yields: ½ cup

Ingredients:

1/3 cup of olive oil

4 capfuls of balsamic vinegar

1 tablespoon Dijon mustard

A squeeze of half lemon

1/8 teaspoon of oregano

1/8 teaspoon of basil

1/8 teaspoon of parsley

A heaping teaspoon of sugar

1/8 teaspoon of salt

1/8 teaspoon of freshly ground pepper

Directions:

Add all the ingredients to a jar with a lid and shake until it is thoroughly mixed.

Chive Vinaigrette

A delicious recipe made with herbs.

Preparation time: 10 minutes

Yields: 8 cups

Ingredients:

8 cups of fresh herb and salad greens (tender stems and leaves).

2 tablespoons of extra-virgin olive oil

1 tablespoon of diced fresh chives

2 teaspoons of white wine vinegar

Half of a small garlic clove, finely diced

Freshly ground black pepper

Kosher salt

Directions:

1. In a large bowl, mix the garlic with a pinch of salt and mash the combination into a paste with a fork.

2. Add the vinegar, oil and chives. Then add salt and pepper to season.

3. Finally, add the herbs and salad greens and toss everything to coat.

Raspberry Vinaigrette

Made with the delicious taste of raspberry and honey.

Preparation time: 5 minutes

Yields: 1 cup

Ingredients:

¼ cup of fresh or frozen raspberries

¼ cup of olive oil

½ cup of white wine vinegar

2 teaspoons of honey

Directions:

Add all the ingredients to a food processor or blender and blend until it becomes very smooth.

Italian Herb Vinaigrette

Combine your vegetables to make this authentic salad dressing.

Preparation time: 10 minutes

Yields: 1½ - 2 cups

Ingredients:

1 cup of roughly chopped fresh flat leaf parsley

¾ cup of extra-virgin olive oil

¼ cup of red wine vinegar

¼ teaspoon of dried oregano

1 ½ teaspoons of honey

10 large fresh basil leaves

2 medium-sized garlic cloves, roughly diced

Kosher salt

Freshly ground black pepper

Directions:

1. Put all the ingredients except the olive oil, salt and pepper in a food processor and allow it run until it forms a smooth paste.

2. Add the oil slowly while the processor is running on low stream. Stop when everything is thoroughly combined and season with salt and pepper.

Easy Lemon Vinaigrette
…Just a simple lemon recipe.

Preparation time: 10 minutes

Yields: 1/3 cup

Ingredients:

3 tablespoons of extra-virgin olive oil

2 tablespoons of lemon juice, freshly squeezed

1 teaspoon of sugar

½ teaspoon of lemon zest, finely grated

½ teaspoon of Dijon mustard

¼ teaspoon of sea salt

Freshly ground black pepper

Directions:

1. Combine the lemon juice, sugar, lemon zest, mustard and sea salt in a small bowl. Whisk everything together until the sugar and salt dissolves.

2. Add the olive oil slowly while whisking. Stop when everything is thoroughly combined and season with salt and pepper.

Basil Strawberry Vinaigrette

This delicious recipe can be a colorful addition to your summer salads.

Preparation time: 5 minutes

Yields: ½ - 1 cup

Ingredients:

1 cup of strawberries, stemmed

1 tablespoon of fresh lemon juice

1 tablespoon of balsamic vinegar

1 tablespoon of extra-virgin olive oil

1 large handful of fresh basil

¼ teaspoon of salt

Freshly ground black pepper

Directions:

Add all the ingredients to a food processor or blender and blend until it becomes very smooth.

Vanilla Raspberry Vinaigrette

Thrill your guests with this yummy summertime treat.

Preparation time: 5 minutes

Yields: 1½ - 1¾ cups

Ingredients:

½ cup of fresh or frozen raspberries

6 oz. of olive oil

2 oz. of water

2 oz. of apple cider vinegar

1 teaspoon of vanilla extract

I teaspoon of sugar

½ teaspoon of salt

Directions:

1. Put all the ingredients except the olive oil in a blender and blend until it combines thoroughly.

2. Add the oil slowly while the blender is running on medium speed.

Blackberry Vinaigrette

Add a twist of blackberry to create the perfect summer vinaigrette.

Preparation time: 10 minutes

Yields: 1- 1½ cup

Ingredients:

1 cup of fresh or frozen blackberries

1/3 cup of red wine vinegar

¼ cup of water

3 tablespoons of olive oil

1 tablespoon of maple syrup

Salt

Pepper

Directions:

1. Place the water and blackberries in a blender or food processor and allow it run until it forms a smooth paste. Strain the paste through a fine sieve to filter out the seeds.

2. Mix the paste with the rest of the ingredients in a jar with a lid and shake thoroughly until it is well-combined.

Concluded!

Made in the USA
Columbia, SC
28 November 2020